Simple Sales Solutions

Self-Motivational Training Guide
to Ensure Success

by

Sheryl Green

Simple Sales Solutions

Self-Motivational Training Guide to Ensure Success

Copyright © 2013 Sheryl Green

Book editing by Felicia Weiss
Book design by Tony Cecala

Printed in the United States of America
First Printing: January 2013

Dedication

I want to dedicate this book to two of the strongest
women I have ever met. One is my Grandmother Dora,
who came to this country from Europe with her
husband, my grandfather, and their four children. When
they arrived in California, my grandfather became ill
and died. My grandmother moved to Houston, Texas
and, with a loan from other immigrant families, she
opened a retail store. She lived next door and woke
before dawn to feed her children before she sent them off
to school. Then she spent her days working in the store.
It was a dry goods store, meaning that she sold food and
basic clothing. She was able to make a livelihood from
that store to support herself and her family.

My mother is the other "steel magnolia." She fled with
her mother and sister, hiding in forests until they were
finally able to find passage to this country. She went to
work after school in a retail store to help support the
family, as she was the oldest. My mother's passion was to
own land. She put any small amount she had toward
owning real estate. She was only able to get a loan for
the real estate she bought if my father could borrow the
money from the bank. He did so reluctantly, grumbling
that she was sending us all to the poor house with her
ability to take money and turn it into dirt (real dirt) like

land. My mother's dirt eventually turned into profit for us so we did not have to go to the poor house. I was really relieved because, from my father's description, I assumed the poor house was not one we wanted to live in.

I also dedicate this book to my father, who taught me about sales. He ran the retail store my grandmother started and I stayed in the store after school until I was 10-years-old. It was there that I watched him sell goods to people. I also watched the people. It was fascinating to me to see the interaction between the customers and my father. Sometimes people would come into the store just to talk to him. They would stay a while and buy something and come back the next day and do the same thing. If my father left to eat lunch or run an errand, they would want to know when he would be back. They would return because they wanted to buy from him.

-Sheryl Green

Contents

Preface

I am writing this book to help those of you who want to learn how to sell or who simply want to be better salespeople. When I started my sales career over thirty years ago, sales training was not as prevalent as it is today. I turned to books to help me learn. I was in a small shop when I decided to try my hand at selling. I was selling gift items and there were over 5,000 items in that gift line. I asked to see the manager. The clerk in front was happy to say that he was there and for me to knock on his door as his office was in the back of the store and up a few stairs. When I realized that I was really going to make a presentation, I became nervous. By the time I reached the manager's office and knocked on the door, I was so anxious that when he asked me to come in, the doorknob slipped out of my hand. The door flew open and hit the wall rather loudly. I was so embarrassed that I said my greeting too loudly and the manager jumped up from his desk and ran to the middle of his shop, waved his arms and asked, "Where is the fire?"

I was hunched against the wall by the door and when he looked at me, I was totally mortified and frightened at the same time. I took in a breath of air and when I could speak, I said in a small voice, "I wanted to see if you

needed some really lovely gift items for your shop."
Needless to say, neither of us were in the mood to
continue along those lines so he politely asked me to
return another time with an appointment.

I realized then that before a sales career could work for
me, it was necessary for me to learn the basic
fundamentals of the selling process. I turned to the
library and while I was standing in front of a row of
books, one fell out and hit me on the foot. It was called,
The Greatest Salesman in the World and it was written by Og
Mandino. The book did not tell me how to sell, but it
did help me to understand that there is far more to the
selling process than mere words. Many times in my
career, I remembered the part of Mandino's book where
he tells of the bird perched outside of his window, where
there were bread crumbs. One day the bird stopped
coming to the window and Mandino never saw it gain.
Soon after another bird came to the window and if the
window was closed, he would tap on the pane with his
beak. Mandino immediately opened the window and let
the fat little Robin inside to eat his breadcrumbs. That
fat little Robin continued to come to the window for
years. If the window was closed, the bird tapped on the
pane and if the window was open he jumped inside to
get fed. It did not matter what the position of the
window was. The bird knew it was up to him to get what
he wanted. The lesson I learned from the bird is that if

you do not ask for the sale, then you will never get the sale. Many salespeople make the mistake of not asking for the sale. If you do not ask and expect the sale, then it will never happen.

The formula for success in selling anything is made up of three words. Those words are PATIENCE, PERSISTENCE AND PERSEVERANCE. Talent in anything is God given and is sometimes well used and sometimes abused. Talent alone will not make you a successful anything, unless you combine that talent with character traits like discipline, patience and determination to succeed. All of these things together, combined with knowledge, make you powerful. This book will give you the knowledge and the inspiration to keep trying until you not only succeed, but exceed your highest aspirations. Selling is a game of life. It is all about you against you.

Keep a steady course.

Remember…the road is long and winding!

Mind not those who would chide and make light of your hopes and dreams that grow from your goals!

Keep your destination in sight.

Introduction

My selling career started more than thirty years ago. I have written this book for those of you who are either starting into sales or who are building onto your current career.

For both men and women selling is necessary for industry to survive today. Sales training is a key essential element, if not for any other reason than to give people an understanding of what the progression is, so they will have a formula to follow. They have to learn something to go on until they have given themselves a chance to master this profession. So come on into your future with me—and all those other staunch souls out there—who are successful in sales.

Remember, nothing happens until a good salesperson motivates and explains the value of his or her product or service.

Part 1: Setting the Stage

Selling is an exchange of energies.

CHAPTER I

What is Professional Selling?

Congratulations! By opening this book, you are about to learn something that may well be the most important advice you will ever gain. Sales training can provide a future for you that can give you the greatest measure of security you have ever had. As if that weren't enough, this training can provide you with a respected place in your community and give you time to yourself for your own personal growth and progress. Besides, selling provides interesting employment, with a great measure of satisfaction by helping other people meet their needs and wants.

If you learn your lessons well, then your sales training can make you a valuable employee to any firm. These proven training results have shown that trained salespeople lower rates of selling costs to sales made because they show a decreased rate of mistakes. Trained salespeople are more confident about their ability to sell. Therefore, they will naturally show more enthusiasm. As you can see, the benefits form a chain of goodwill from customer to salesperson or product, just because the salesperson is more secure in his or her job.

The era of being an order-taker is over. Buyers are now more well-informed and want professional, intelligent salespeople to help them. Selling is a very rewarding career, and your top-notch salespeople regard it just that way ... AS A CAREER . . . not an avocation! They respect their jobs and wisely learn everything they can about selling techniques. This includes their sales material, their marketing area, and their product. They improve their appearance, voice, and attitude, for they know that all of these make the difference between a pro, and the person who is there simply because there was nothing else for him or her to do. The difference between a salesperson and a conversationalist is that the salesperson knows how to open doors, create a need for his or her product or service, and close a sale.

Since this book is for everyone in sales, we are going to stick to our special goals. At this time, let us go to the dictionary definition of selling. Selling means, "To gain acceptance and attract prospective buyers for your product and service. The end result of that is to exchange ownership for money or its equivalent." This is a simple statement, but how to do all of that is what you will know when you have finished the study of this book. The cliche that all salespeople are born with that talent, and those who are successful in sales are just lucky, has been dismissed by every professional in the sales field today. Salespeople have to be trained for their profession.

As a sales professional, your job is a technical one that requires developed skill. Before you will be given the opportunity to sell your merchandise and your company, you must first sell yourself. This means that you must first of all believe in all three: yourself, your product and your company. Then, and only then, can you convey that conviction to your customer. Salespeople are not born, but made by systematic study of proven principles of good salesmanship. You must know your job as well as you know your name.

We will go through the seven building blocks of your sale later, after you have learned the foundation on which to build that sale. You must know your product or merchandise thoroughly. This includes price, size, and all you can technically know about each and every item that you are selling. Let's face it, most customers want you to help sell them what fits their needs. They don't want to take the time from their day to go through every item or concept you have. They will wait until the right salesperson comes along, who has the idea or item in front of them, presents it to them succinctly, smoothly and quickly. You must also learn to know your customers, and what they are looking for in the things they buy. Some want to buy for price, some for design, and some for durability; so do a little research on your customers. Find out what they want. Knowing what the other person wants is called empathy.

Going back to the dictionary definition, empathy is, "An understanding so attuned that you readily comprehend the thoughts, actions, and motives of the other person." When you can put yourself in the other person's shoes, then you can successfully convince that person that you are sincerely trying to help him or her. This is what selling is all about—helping people get what they want. When you have gained the respect and confidence of your customer, and he or she relies on your judgment, then no competitor or even a cheaper product will ever take that account away from you.

1. Selling requires gaining acceptance so that you can attract prospective buyers. It is finding out what the customer wants and giving it to them.

2. Selling helps other people understand their wants and needs.

3. Selling is a technical job, requiring training.

4. Trained salespeople are more confident. They are more enthusiastic and THEY MAKE MORE SALES.

The Fashions of the times are the visual chronicle of society's growth.

We are what we perceive ourselves to be at a given time...

Visually we show this perception in our clothing.

Our attitude shows
in our speech.

CHAPTER II

Your Professionalism Shows...

Three things form the basis on which a prospective buyer will make his or her decision about whether to let you take his or her time and allow you the space to relate to your sales pitch. The way you appear to the prospective buyer is of immediate importance… APPEARANCE counts! This includes your grooming, cleanliness, and the way that you dress. The next attribute that gives an impression is your MIND CAPACITY FOR SUCCESS! That means how well you have prepared yourself mentally for the sale and how well you convey your interest in your career. The third quality of judgment, and certainly not the least important, is ATTITUDE! The attitude you show about what you are doing is the real difference between the pro and the beginner. Some salespeople, who have been selling for twenty years or more, are still beginners in this category. "Why?" The reason is more attitude reflected…about their employer, their job, and, yes, even themselves.

How important are these traits in the real scheme of things? The answer is: They are more important than the skills you learn to make your sale, for these are the attributes that show who and what you really are. It is still a fact that people buy from people they like. We are now going to systematically explain why and how to show the very best of you.

a. APPEARANCE

The first step in professionalism is visual appearance. Just how important appearance is to selling cannot be stressed enough. At times your appearance is the only quality that will or will not allow you the opportunity to sell. Visual appearance lets the prospective buyer gain a perception of the salesperson. This visual perception that the prospective buyer receives of the salesperson may well make the difference between making the sale to that person or not even being able to say, "Hello"! You must work at looking professional for you are a performer. Just as much as an actor or actress is on stage every working day, so are you.

First of all, be sure that your clothing is brushed and clean. Allow enough time in the morning to inspect your appearance very carefully before you leave. Watch for cleanliness. Do not wear faddish styles. For example certain styles may be too faddish for your business hour activities. If there is the slightest doubt about a blouse with a spot on it, or an outfit that needs pressing, have it cleaned or, if prohibitive, just pressed. For fragrance, a light and airy scent is preferable, nothing overwhelming.

Check your fingernails. Make sure they are clean. Ladies, if your nail polish is chipping, then cover it or take it off completely. When you are showing a product or an idea in a manual every day, then you are showing your hands also. Be sure that you would want someone else to see what your fingernails look like.

Next, your hair style should be comfortable and attractive. Keep your styling free and easy, rather than elaborate. Too much fussiness in hair styling should be saved for times when you can relax with friends. You must remember that you are trying to instill confidence in you from people who have never even seen you before. Try to keep your wardrobe to a tailored look. If it is not that way now, then replenish with tailored blouses and skirts as you need something new. To keep the cost of a wardrobe down, stay with a single color scheme as much as possible. You will accomplish two things by having a classic wardrobe; first, it will allow you to have the right look for any situation; and second, with a single color scheme, you can accessorize and mix and match to change your look frequently. This will allow you to spend more on a single item since you will not need to buy as many. Remember, you are the star on the stage when you are selling. Everything you say or do or wear expresses who you are and what you represent. A buyer wants to deal with successful people and their appearance is the first clue.

b. MENTAL PREPARATION

Mind training and discipline in selling is more important than any other aspect you need to conquer. I firmly believe that what you can train your mind to believe is what will ultimately happen. Several years ago when we went into a recession, the newspapers were filled with all kinds of depressing reports. One day, while reading the financial news over a cup of coffee, one of those really successful older, seasoned salesmen came along and closed my newspaper. "Why did you do that?" I asked him.

His answer is something that I will always remember: "Salespeople bring their own mental climate with them. If they read depressing news, then they may bring that along also." All successful salespeople have a challenging and optimistic outlook. They have learned to completely remove negative thoughts from their minds and constantly picture themselves in successful situations.

A classic story to illustrate this is that of the math student, who arrived late for his exam. The teacher had already given the instructions. The class had begun. The student just rushed in, took his paper, and proceeded to his desk to begin. Well, alas, when the class time was over, he wasn't finished. He asked the teacher if he could take the rest of the problems home and finish them there. The instructor agreed, but told him that the test had to be returned by 6:00pm. The student struggled with the remaining problems for hours, but when it came time to return the paper, he had solved all but one of the problems. He turned the test in anyway and proceeded home. An excited professor phoned the student at 3:00am the following morning unable to control his excitement as the words came tumbling out. It seems when the instructions were given, the students were told to solve as many of the math problems as they could: for there were three of the problems that had never been solved: In fact, they were considered unsolvable. The student who was late did not hear this information. He therefore THOUGHT that the test was like any other one, where all of the problems had to be solved. It appears that this student had solved problems that had never been solved before simply because HE THOUGHT HE COULD!

You would be amazed at how a few minutes of visualizing yourself reaching a goal each and every day of your life makes the attainment of that goal easier and easier for you. Train your mind in this way to set sales goals for yourself each and every day. If you do this daily, these goals will, by necessity, have to be set higher and higher. This is a law of nature. Since we live in a magnetic universe, we automatically attract that which we concentrate our energies on. So visualize the attainment of your own goals as part of the homework you do each and every day before you go out to sell.

c. ATTITUDE

Your attitude shows more about how you feel about what you are doing than perhaps anything in relation to your presentation to the customer. Remember how we said that a prospective buyer forms an unconscious opinion about the salesperson from the way that salesperson projects him- or herself? Well, attitude shows, and you project that attitude whether or not you are conscious of this fact.

Attitude makes the difference between success and failure in anything you attempt to do. Consequently, when you leave your home in the morning, leave your personal problems there, too. This takes discipline. Remember that word discipline? You first saw it in the initial pages of this book, as one of the essentials of professional selling. If you want to grumble about your company or another customer (which we all do at times because we are human), then do it on your own time. When you dwell on negative thoughts, then you waste time and energy that you could be putting to good and productive use. This is an important point: Never, I mean never, disclose your professional problems to your customers. Tell it to your sales manager or any other person, who can help you to do something about it. When a salesperson reveals professional problems to customers, the customers stand to lose the confidence they have in that salesperson, as well as respect for the company being represented. If this ever happens, the only real loser in the long run is you. So always maintain good discipline for without it you lose control of the sale: Good salespeople always control the sale.

Customers usually have their own agendas. Sometimes the customer you are with at the time will test you. A lot of them will do this to a new salesperson just to hassle him or her and see what they can say. If the customer does that, then stay on track, make a joke, or, better still, come back with a complimentary remark about that customer. Do you know what this tactic can do? It completely unbalances the buyer and puts you right where you should be—in control of the sale. If the customer tries to unbalance you or test you, then you can counter the situation with a tactful remark, which allows you to keep control of the sales situation. To control the situation at all times is what every new sales rep must learn to do.

I've heard good sales managers tell new reps to take up a sport, such as tennis, jogging or swimming, or even throwing darts as a hobby when they first start to sell. A sport helps to release all of those frustrations that you encounter during the day. It clears your mind, and allows you to see where you or the other person went wrong. It gives you a clearer outlook on life, so that you can maintain that good, positive mental attitude. You get another benefit also if you take up a strenuous sport: You will look better, too. We all want that.

1. The prospective buyer gives the salesperson the right to make the sale to him or her.

2. Attitude is the factor that determines the sale.

3. People buy from people they like.

4. When you look at yourself, at the beginning of the business day, would you want to buy from you?

5. Visualize yourself achieving your sales goals.

6. Keep a positive mental outlook. You bring the climate of the sale with you.

The ability to serve is the gift that God gives to the life of the individual!

CHAPTER III

Giving and Getting

Today, especially when high technology is the rule in all manufacturing processes, the only thing that one company has to offer over another is service. The type of service you give depends on what you are selling. That simply goes back to doing a little research to learn the marketing area that this product will reach. Try to put yourself in the place of the consumer of this product or service. What questions would you have? Try to make your customer aware of these questions and try to answer some of them at the outset before you leave the customer's place of business. The only way to do this is to ask questions. Sometimes service is just a question of degree of inquiry into how fast the items need to be replaced. In addition, develop your marketing area by doing some research into your customer's habits. Try to figure the turnover that your items will have if you are selling consumable goods.

- Be there when your customer needs you.

- Always return calls promptly.

- Solve problems efficiently.

Believe me, the only thing some companies have going for them is the service their salespeople give. Giving good service today can be as simple as a follow-up phone call or as generous as a gesture to show that you really care about your company and the people who are their customers and yours as well.

A good example of service, requiring patience, persistence and perseverance, which led to success, is illustrated in the story of a lady, who owned a small gift shop. Many years ago when I first started to sell gift items door to door to small gift shops, I met a lady in her small shop. I had just started in my career and was very excited to be able to show those wonderful items to all who would be able to display them and sell them to their customers. When I walked into her small store, she was behind the counter. I immediately and proudly introduced myself and received a not so welcoming response. In fact, the lady was very angry with my company, as my predecessor had not been diligent in following up to see that her order arrived in good condition. It seems that some of the items she had ordered came in broken and the previous salesman had not responded, so the items were never replaced.

Well, I came along, a new salesperson, who knew nothing about what had happened and I received the brunt of the lady's anger. In fact, she was so angry that she would not listen to my apology and, ultimately, she asked me to leave. I did, but I did not feel right about what had happened to her. A few days later I was in the neighborhood again and I decided to go back and try to talk to this lady. I thought that perhaps I could offer her some of the samples that I had. I had to pay for the samples, but I thought it was the right thing to do, given the loss she had had from the items that were broken. I felt that the least I could do to show her that I cared was to offer her something to replace what was damaged.

When I entered her store she was there, busily fixing a display. When she turned around, she gave me a look that could have melted a diamond. I sputtered and really wanted to melt into my very tailored jacket, but I persisted. She said, "Didn't I ask you to leave a few days ago?"

I said that was true, but I wanted her to know that I felt badly that she had had such a bad experience with the company I was representing. I told her that I could not offer her much, but that I had some samples and I wanted her to have them for free. Well, she sat down and stared at me for what seemed like an hour (although it was really only a minute). What happened next was surprising even to me. She asked me to sit down, take out an order form and go through her inventory with her. She placed one of the largest orders that I had had

to date. This was very significant as it was only my first
month in sales.

In fact, she became one of my best customers. More
importantly, she was my best advertisement. Anyone that
she knew, who needed items for their store, she referred
to me. I learned many great lessons from this. First and
foremost, people want to know that you care about them
and the experience they have with your product and/or
service. The second thing I learned was that word of
mouth and the reputation you carry with you can make
or break you as a salesperson. Most important of all was
that real service pays off in dollars.

A good salesperson not only studies the marketing trends
and inquires into the welfare of the customer, but
actually does everything they can to help their
customers. By inquiring into the minds of your
customer, you show that you care about them. Many
times we do not know how much a kind word or an
uplifting phrase can help someone. You, as a salesperson,
provide the motivation and inspiration that makes the
sale happen and consistently keeps the sale going. When
you constantly communicate you find out what the
customer is thinking.

Recently, I was able to help someone with their brand
new home. They were confident, excited, and nervous,

all at the same time. Something then happened to delay the sale and cause a problem with the loan that the buyers were trying to get. When I found out about it, I was able to give them some insight into the process. I was also able to use my experience in the business to tell them about other people, who have had a challenging experience procuring a loan. I simply said, "This happens quite frequently and you, as buyers, have done exactly what you need to do."

The next day I found out that the buyers were able to continue with the process and, recently, they closed on their new home. It wasn't until after they closed that they told me that the very day I had given them words of encouragement, which allowed them to stop worrying about their loan, the missing pieces came together and things worked out. They asked me how I knew that it would happen. My answer was, "A lot of faith and prayer." This taught me that my job does not end when the product or service gets into the hands of the person needing it. The ability to help and serve comes in many different forms.

Whether you spend five minutes inquiring into the welfare of your customer, or hours in research to service an account, the time you spend puts dollars into your pocket. Remember, SERVICE is the only thing you have in this age of high prices that puts you ahead of the competition.

Think of serving your market as a gift you want to give. Remember how good giving made you feel? And serving your customer well is the gift you give back to thank them for buying from you. This gift returns a hundredfold in dollars as well as in warm goodwill. This goodwill makes friends for you. When you wake up in the morning, before you climb out of bed, repeat to yourself or just remind yourself, "I am out there to SERVE my customers." Boy, will this ever make the dollars find you, especially if you say it every day of your selling career. Remember, in sales, as in life, the words "I SERVE," will serve you.

SERVICE ...

1. Service requires you to think of the other person.

2. Efficiency is a by-product of service.

3. Service is what makes people buy from one person and not from another.

Life is a journey...

Never a destination.

CHAPTER IV

How to Approach

Just as there is a natural process of growing that takes place when a baby becomes a young child, then matures into a teenager, so there is a natural process of growth for adults, who learn something new. There is first that confusing time of the "me" part of learning. "Who am I? Where do I stand in this new situation?" Next comes, "How do I relate to this new world around me?" That is precisely where we are now! The "me" and the what-is-expected-of-me phase is over and we are going to interrelate. You are presently a salesperson in your profession relating as such. Selling is made up of a visual, perceptual and verbal presentation. In part A, we concentrated mainly on the visual and verbal. However, all three of the above are of equal importance in the presentation. Otherwise, brochures could very well replace salespeople. However, they never will for two very precise and necessary ingredients are necessary: The perceptual and the visual-verbal reaction.

In wanting to be thorough at this point, I am led into an explanation of an area of space used by human beings, which they silently hold claim to: "Territory." People relate to space more seriously than one would expect. It is a silent statement of respect to some and position to others.

Recently in a meeting someone had put an item on a table in front of a chair where people would sit in the meeting. Unknowingly, a lady sat down in the seat near the object on the table. The meeting started and another woman walked in and verbalized her anger at losing "her spot". She actually threatened to get that spot back.

We all, even the most nonaggressive of us, claim a certain space as our own. How certain people relate and aggress to other people's zones tells a lot about how they can relate to their world and to other individuals. The science of how the zones of territories are of use to us in sales is important to know.

The three zones in which humans relate are "Intimate Distance," "Personal Zone," and "Public Space." Each of these is then subdivided further. "Intimate Distance" is for close and far intimate distance. "Personal Zone" has a far and close space. "Public Space" can be far and close. The following will explain each of these distances and how they can be used most comfortably and successfully in our society:

A.   INTIMATE DISTANCE

1. Close: This is actual contact with another, or as far as six to eighteen inches away. This distance is embarrassing to two people, who are not intimate. Surprisingly, two women in our culture can comfortably be this distance away from each other. However, in our culture for two men to be this close to each other would feel like an invasion of territory.

2. Far: This distance is eighteen inches away. Again, surprisingly enough, this far-intimate distance is considered all right for men and women at cocktail parties. This far-intimate distance is always awkward to men in our society. To observe this, watch two men in a crowded subway or elevator, who are pushed this close to each other: They will stiffen their bodies and try to pull away.

B.   PERSONAL ZONE

1. Close: This is from one and one-half to two and one-half feet away. A husband and wife are comfortable with each other at this distance. Were anyone else to get this close to either the husband or wife, then both would view this as an invasion of territory.

2.   Far: The far phase of personal zone is from two and one-half to four feet. This is what we see as acceptable when acquaintances meet and stop to chat. At this distance, the person leaves an area of politeness.

To move closer on a far-personal relationship will denote pushiness on the part of the intruder. The salesperson should make mental note of this especially.

C.   SOCIAL AND PUBLIC SPACE

1. Close: The close social distance is from four to seven feet away. The social spacing can be used by salespeople when they approach a client by stopping and greeting them at this distance.

2. Far: The far social zone is from seven to twelve feet away. This sometimes is called the power space. It is where the person in charge can stay to denote their importance. A manager or person in charge maintains this distance and sometimes gets an entire view of the area of responsibility in their environment.

If you, as a salesperson, understand these unspoken statements, then you can more quickly qualify your buyer in regard to degree of importance. When speaking with two people, who are making a decision about whether to buy or not to buy, notice who stands further back and is the most silent. Most of the time it is the person who stands apart and is silent, who is the decision maker. So do not be fooled that you have impressed the outgoing, talkative one as this person may not be the one who makes the buying decision. The unspoken gestures in our society can save you a lot of effort in evaluating the time you need to spend with the person.

This zone of space is important for still another reason: It is here that you as a salesperson should pause, make your initial greeting, and wait for the nod or verbal response from your customer before you proceed into his or her environment. If you practice and know this area well, then at times you can lead the potential buyer into the office or area of doing business.

The pointers about how we use space in our society are other tools of knowledge that you can practice and use to save you time and make you money. Remember, in the first part of this book, I told you that selling would help you in your personal life, as well as enlarge your understanding and therefore your ability to know other people. Now add to that: The more you know not only about your product, but about other people, the more successful you will be in sales, and the more dollars you will add to your bank account.

When you do something consciously every day, you soon develop a habit of doing the same thing, and it becomes part of your subconscious. That is why it is important to learn everything you can so that you develop a physical and procedural awareness of everything you are doing. Then you can strive to do it as well as you possibly can.

You will learn to evaluate the requests of your customers, and will, as a natural sequence in the course of your pursuit, learn to comply with their needs, without letting a customer take advantage of you. You must learn to maintain a friendly manner, a pleasant voice, and a smile, but do draw the line at letting yourself be used by the customer.

Just as we discussed how you are to leave your personal problems when you walk out your front door, so too, do you walk into someone else's problems when you walk into their front door. Customers like to believe they are your friends and in a sense they are; however, they are your professional friends.

I will illustrate this with a story. A salesperson, who is very good in his field, took over an account that had belonged to a young man, who was new in the business. When the seasoned salesperson called the account, the lady, who was the buyer, started sobbing and explained that Tony (the young man who was new in the business), had become her best friend and she was devastated to learn that he was no longer going to be her salesperson. Further into the conversation the seasoned salesperson realized that not only had Tony spent his whole day with that one account, he also noticed that the account was draining the company's profits. The account had convinced the salesperson to spend too much time and too much of the company's resources doing something that the company could not make a profit on because it was out of the realm of their capabilities. Why did this happen? We as sales people are vulnerable. Other people have their agendas as well. We should never let our goals be overridden by someone, who knowingly or not, will take advantage of us. The new salesperson in the above example did not realize his role.

There is a fine balance between helping someone and being taken advantage of. Had Tony listened to the customer, taken her situation into consideration, given her a solution within the guidelines of the capabilities of the company, then everyone would have won. In this situation Tony let the customer take advantage of him and his company because he did not explain clearly the boundaries. As salespeople we all have the tendency to want to help people; however, (and this is big), if you let the customer control the situation, then you both lose.

Always keep in mind that your role as a salesperson is to promote your product, let the customer know the extent of what you can and cannot do, and make it valuable to the customer so that they will choose you as a professional to help them. It does no good to give empty promises as they lead to unhappy customers and lots of backtracking. So remember to say, "No" when you cannot do something. The customer will respect you for it.

Sometimes there is a fine line between being friendly and getting to know someone, and letting that someone use your time to tell you his or her personal problems. Too much of this takes time away from your next sale, where you should be to make money. The single most valuable negotiable item a salesperson has is time. Serve your market well and thoroughly, but use your time productively and wisely.

MOVING INTO THE TERRITORY:

1. Acceptable distances are different for two women, than they are for two men, or for a man and a woman.

2. Business situations dictate a different set of rules concerning distance than social situations do.

3. Distance is used to signify importance in a group or organization.

4. Orders are written and signed in a particular space in your prospective buyer's place of business. Find it before you start the sale.

5. A salesperson's time and space used well means money.

Fear detains.

Conversely...

Faith sustains.

CHAPTER V

There's Magic in the Movement

I was a model in the clothing market and I watched salespeople sell. I did this for years, in my young teens and early twenties. I was so impressed and fascinated with the way these salespeople could take a nonplussed customer from indifferent disdain to a subservient, loyal customer. I used to call it magic. It is that, but it is also so much more.

By the tradition of progression, nothing happens in any sale until trust is established on both sides. The most basic explanation of selling is that a sale is made when a salesperson has a strong belief in what he or she is selling and has the ability to transfer that belief to the person doing the buying. When that has taken place, the good salesperson can feel that magic move, for even the energies surrounding the sales situation change. That is the time the people involved in the sale decide to trust each other. It is not until this trust is established, and the transference of belief has begun, that the sales process can actually begin.

The actual selling process is a series of advances and hesitations. What is actually happening is that the salesperson is nudging for the close, and the customer is responding with language that says, "I trust you," or, "Give me more time to trust." This exchange is the most important part of the selling process and should never be rushed. If this portion of the sale is not done thoroughly, the salesperson has to go back to reinforce feelings of trust that should have already been established.

That is why, at times, when someone is listening (and doesn't know what is going on), the conversation sounds fragmented. One will hear strong selling points being made and then interjections of personal situations from the prospective buyer. What the prospective buyer is trying to do at this time is to establish his or her own conviction to buy. For the salesperson this stage takes another one of those key words—Patience. This is something that we need to practice daily. At this point in the sale, we need to be patient in the right way.

That is why often the salesperson will want to go back over the selling points and reinforce the trust. This should be done as many times as is needed. This questioning phase gives the opportunity to test the bond that is being woven on the way to the conclusion of the sale. It is necessary to continue in the process of establishing trust until it is firmly bonded for the successful conclusion of the sale. Remember, a slow response is only a careful reaching out in an attempt to trust. Enough practice in this phase of the sale gives the seasoned sales professional what we refer to as a "sixth sense." The good salesperson can then make the decision as to whether or not the sale will be closed, by the exchange that has gone on in this phase.

Selling is an opportunity that a salesperson can give themselves. It gives a salesperson the chance to achieve by using those innate qualities that belong to him or her. Selling does not ask more of the individual than he or she is prepared to give. By the same token, it can absorb more as the individual is ready to give more. There is true magic in this. Selling then does not ask more of you than you want to give, conversely, selling gives back all and more than is given. It is a progression, something that can grow within the individual. People cannot live totally unto themselves. They must share life with others. Selling asks only that you share what you are with life.

The magic in anything is trust:

1. When the person selling can transfer his or her belief in what he or she is doing to another, then a sale is made.

2. The ability to instill trust in another is a technical skill that can be learned.

3. Patience is the key to making and keeping the sale and the customer.

4. Selling is one of the opportunities in life that lets a person use that which is the sum total of the personality in a gainful endeavor.

5. Since so much of the individual goes into the sale, it can be an extremely creative and rewarding personal experience.

It is with diligence that deeds become acts...

Acts practiced over a period of time become character

CHAPTER VI

Going Along with the Situation... Until the Situation Goes Along with You

We stated before that every buyer puts up a wall of resistance to every new sales rep who walks in. It is up to you to break through that wall as smoothly and as quickly as you can. You do want your customer to like to buy from you, for people buy from people they like. That is why in the time you give after the greeting and the approach, you want to be as courteous and friendly as possible: To enable you to get that customer to trust you and like you enough to listen to what you have to offer. Remember to let potential customers talk about themselves; everyone loves to talk about personal interests.

Your goal at this time is to break through that invisible wall as smoothly and as quickly as possible. Make every question you ask a leading question and one that will give you back information as to what the customer is looking for, who your competition is, and what motivates this particular customer to buy. Avoid any question that can be answered with a simple, "Yes", or "No". Think

back a few pages when we said that the good salesperson
controls the sale at all times.

This is your best opportunity to do just that. It is up to
you at this time to lead the conversation quickly and
efficiently to what you need to know to effectively make
the sale. At this point you will sometimes get all sorts of
negative comments, such as, your competitor's line is
cheaper, better, or more efficient in some ways than
yours. Believe it or not, this is an opportunity. It means
that you have gotten through that artificial wall and the
customer is opening up with interest in you and in what
you have to say. The excuses that your competition is
better, cheaper, gives a faster turnover, etc., is just a test
to see how informed you, as the salesperson, are about
your market and how well you keep control of the selling
situation. So, realize this is an opening to answer about
your major competition.

Learn the major sellers that compete with you in their
product line, their quality, their prices, their marketing
area, etc. This immediately gives you an edge for you
will be able to come back with an answer that is
complimentary to your line. You are left in control of the
sale, still, for you will retain your confidence by knowing
the answers and can make that buyer dwell on the good
points you wish to bring out.

Never, I mean never, try to run down your competition. When you do this with a buyer, whom you do not know well and who does not know you, then you are putting that buyer on the defensive. He or she will try to prove to him- or herself and to you that he or she was smart to put in the competitor's line. At that point you not only do not gain, but you actually lose the sale for all time. The less you say about another product line, the better off you are. When you talk about another's business, you bring their label to mind and end up giving free advertisement. So, concentrate your time and energies on that which is positive and beneficial to you. Devote your sales talk to appropriate and true facts about each thing you wish to sell.

Earlier in this book we said to always assume that your buyer is going to buy. The way to sell something is not "If" they will buy, but "Which one" or "How many" they will buy. Always assume when buyers question an item that they are going to buy that item or something similar. People do not question things in which they have no interest.

The best way to know when to go into the actual sale is to use your own intuitive sense. The common sense courtesy of listening attentively to what the other person is saying is what you have to really make a practice of doing, especially when you are new at the selling game.

It is right here in the questioning stage that salespeople can give up. However, selling is a technical process and any technical process can be learned.

Just picture this stage of the selling process as a game of racquetball or tennis that you are involved in. You would miss the next shot if you didn't concentrate closely on what was going on in the game. Not only is the game of selling on the line when you are at this stage, but the game of finance is as well. The stakes are as high as you set them. The rewards go to the victor. Every objection that you counter, every stroke that you give to the buyer, should be done with a goal in sight. That goal is to win the sale. Just think, as you master your profession, you can mentally give yourself a trophy every time the sale is won!

As a salesperson, you have to take the information that is given to you when you ask those leading questions and at the same time know your line well enough to come up with some pretty quick ideas that will make the sale for you. Pretty tricky, huh? However, pros do it every day with each and every sale they make. This intuition is the one thing that most good, professional salespeople cannot explain, for it involves a great amount of creativity.

If you have never heard this before, you will be surprised to learn that most good salespeople are extremely creative people. They have to learn to take the tools that they have to work with (their selling materials) and fit what they have into each and every situation that they come across. Of course, (using that old common sense thing again), you must put yourself into a situation that is advantageous to you and what you have to sell. This positioning goes back to doing a little market research before you start to sell whatever you are going to sell.

* With practice, you will get better and achieve your own style of selling. It will he easier each time to quickly come up with the item or idea that will start you into the selling process.

* Salespeople become very perceptive as they mingle with the same type of people in their own area of expertise every day: So if you use that empathy (an understanding so attuned that you can readily put yourself in the other person's shoes), and your creativity, then you have all the tools you need to effectively create the opening so that you can make your sale.

* Be sure your selling aids are assembled and available so that when it is time to go into the sale, you do not fumble and distract the customer.

* Your goal in selling is to transact your business with a minimum of confusion and effort, both for the etiquette of other people's time (their time is as valuable to them as yours is to you), and so that you can finish that transaction in the shortest possible time. This also helps you to not give the customer a chance to change course.

* The preceding chapter was for one reason, and one reason only, to encourage you to make a sale tailored for that particular account.

1. The best way to find out about other people is to let them tell you about themselves.

2. The salesperson who knows how to listen will learn exactly what the prospective buyer wants.

3. The more people talk about themselves, the more they like the person who is listening to them.

4. Listen well and close as quickly as possible as the meeting time for salesperson and buyer is so brief that a transaction should be made while energies are attuned.

Our Shadow goes before us and leaves when we do...

Our Reputation goes with us and stays l-o-n-g after we are gone.

CHAPTER VII

Keep the Confidence

Guess what? You are into the body of the sale and that happened just as easily as you knew it would. From the feedback in conversation, you realized what that particular customer's problems were ... and what motivated the sale and you studied your product line or selling tools so well that you have come up with the very product that will be useful to that account. You must know this without searching the prices, sizes, and different ways that your products can relate to that account.

When you are selling as a professional, one very important thing to remember is, to the best of your ability, do not ever tell someone that you can do something that you will not or can not. This is especially important when you are beginning to sell and build a reputation; do not try to lie your way through a situation. Believe me, you will get so much support and help from people if you honestly admit that you are new to your situation. Ask these same customers to help you with the answers. People love to help others and to show how much they know.

One of the biggest sales I ever made was by letting a customer know that I was new to the business. I did it by asking for help so that I would know more about that situation and their particular problems. Let people know that you are sincere in wanting to know all you can about them, so that you are better able to serve them. The other side of this is for you to learn as quickly as you can, for people will run out of patience with someone, who takes their valuable time.

Sometimes, and especially at this time in the economy, popular items in every line are out of stock or difficult to get. Don't discourage the sale by stating point blank that you are out of something that the buyer wants. Instead, get the buyer to concentrate on and to like something similar that you can get more easily. However, be honest and if you actually are backed into a corner and are told that there is only one item the customer wants, tell the customer the truth and explain why it is difficult to get that particular product. Most of the time people will understand and then allow themselves to go on to the available item.

Always assume that when a buyer has his or her attention on a particular item that he or she is going to buy it. Remember, the way to sell is not "If," but "Which" or "How many." At times you can give the buyer options as to size or quantity, but make sure each and every time you give the buyer a choice that whatever he or she chooses favors you. Most people like to think that they made their own choice of what and when to buy: You are out there to give them ideas and to sell goods or services. Always the way to sell is not by using "If" but "How much" and "When to deliver." As you are closer to finishing the sale, you are narrowing in on just a few points and proceeding with writing the order. Continue to keep the customer interested in his or her train of thought as long as you are writing and closing.

Remember, this is not the time to introduce any more new ideas into the mind of the buyer. Wait to do this when you have patiently and thoroughly completed the order. Get that order that you completed signed, then you can try to add on to the sale if you feel that it is still possible. When the customer has finished with his or her train of thought in buying, only then will you introduce any more new ideas. If you hurry the sale, or confuse the customer, then you stand to lose all that you have worked so hard for. Once you have your order, the next step is to pack up your samples and orders and to pleasantly and smoothly leave.

1. Letting another person help brings on a deeper commitment to the situation.

2. Show courtesy and respect for another's time.

3. Clearly and concisely show other people what they are looking for and what will help them.

4. Always assume that the customer will buy. The question in the sale, then is not, "If" but "How many?"

5. Continue the train of thought until the sale is completed.

Time is the Thief of Life

CHAPTER VIII

Leave Them Waiting for More

So you've finished your sale, packed up your samples and order forms and you want to leave. The customer is still talking about business, orders or any such thing, but you need to get on to your next sale. The longer you let this conversation linger, the more chance you have of wasting your time, or the greatest pitfall of all, you risk the order being changed. So pack up, be pleasant, and start to say something about when you will return.

It is at this time that you may have a little tidbit of information about new technology in your field or a new product coming in your line. The subconscious is more powerful than any of us have taken the time to observe, so subconsciously that customer is storing the information you have given and, even if the customer is not conscious of doing it, association of you with that information will be there when you return. Also, let each customer know an approximate time you will return or make contact again. This lets the customers know that you are interested in him or her as well as in your profession. You will be amazed at how often the customer will tell you that you returned at the time that you said you would, or that you were early...or late in checking back. Always remember that the next sale begins when the first one ends.

All right, you are through, all packed up and are leaving. Now it is time to just say good-bye. (This sounds like a song, doesn't it?) Remember to smile! If you haven't learned it yet: The two most important words in our language are: "Thank You." You had better start to learn and practice saying this today. When you leave a buyer's place of business that last impression is just as important as the first impression. If you accomplished your job well, then you will only have to make that first impression once. However, the last impression you will have to make many times so leave with a smile, a "Thank you" and tell them that you appreciate their having bought from you. This courtesy just reinforces that buyer's opinion of him- or herself as being discriminating and intelligent enough to buy from you. The next sale has already started; you just finished this one.

1. When the sale is complete, leave them hanging on and waiting for the next sale.

2. Give a definite period of time that the customer knows he or she will see you again.

3. Always leave courteously and let the customer know that you appreciate the sale.

SUMMARY

To summarize the points you have read about so far in this book in successful and professional selling, let us once more list those qualities that make up successful selling. These, after all, are the foundation stones that you put in place to build a career.

A. DESIRE TO SERVE

B. KNOWLEDGE OF MERCHANDISE OR PRODUCT AND COMPETITION

C. SELLING SKILLS

D. ENTHUSIASM

E. LOYALTY TO YOUR ORGANIZATION

Picture the above statements in your mind. Keep them with you every day when you go out to sell. They will make you a rich and successful individual in so many ways.

Part II: The Seven Building Blocks

The Higher You Go
The Farther
You See

CHAPTER IX

The Seven Building Blocks to the Professional Sale

Now that we have settled on the best possible approach to selling initially, we move on to putting into practice the insights you have been given.

The Seven Building Blocks to the Professional Sale:

BLOCK I: APPROACH AND GREETING

BLOCK II: LEARNING THE CUSTOMER'S WANTS AND NEEDS

BLOCK III: LOCATING AND PRESENTING MERCHANDISE

BLOCK IV: STIMULATING THE DESIRE TO BUY AND CONVINCE

BLOCK V: CLOSE THE SALE

BLOCK VI: ADD ON TO THE SALE

BLOCK VII: THE FOLLOW-UP TO THE SALE

The groundwork is complete, so to speak, and it is now time for us to stack the blocks that will lead you to the attainment of your successful sales. To be able to effectively break the sale down into parts and to know which part you must concentrate on, at the time you are actually into the sale, is something that some professionals know, and have known for years, yet are not aware of.

In any field in which people call themselves professionals, they must know and be aware of every move they make at the exact time they are making it. This knowledge helps salespeople to effectively order their actions so that they will be correct in every point they make. It also helps them in case the sale is not progressing as they would like it to. If this is the case, they can then effectively back track, correct their mistakes, and move forward again. So, you see, the gains made by professionals are well-practiced and solid steps toward the attainment of their goals. When you have completed your study of these seven building blocks to the successful completion of a sale and have practiced them well, then your mistakes will be almost nonexistent as you will have been able to both erase and correct them at the same time.

To me such progress is a very exciting reason to learn these lessons and to learn them well. When you make fewer errors, then you can then use your time so much more effectively. As we have stated before, time is the most valuable tool that a salesperson has. You were led to this point, just as certain events in your life lead you to a place for further growth. Consequently, in the same manner, this approach to selling was carefully sequenced for you. With a step-by-step progression into each and every part of the sale you are making, you will be able to overcome any pitfall or roadblock put in your path.

Once the customer is interested and has given you hints as to what he or she needs and will buy, it is time to show how your product or service will fulfill that need or will solve the buyer's problem. I repeat, when you learn the needs of the customer, then all you have to do is present to him or her what you have to fulfill that need.

In order to stimulate the desire to buy effectively, you, the salesperson, must know your product line or service benefits so well that you do not have to fumble or stumble. If the right product or solution is there at the right moment, you can easily and efficiently show how it fits into the buyer's dream. Then you are practically guaranteed the sale.

To Most People

The Most Interesting Conversations

Are Those About Themselves

CHAPTER X

Approach and Greeting

With your planning complete, your grooming checked, your mental preparation in order, and your knowledge of your product line firmly in your mind, let us go out to meet the customer. The greeting and approach step is sometimes the most crucial one. At this point, the customer decides whether he or she will allow you, the salesperson, to take up his or her time. Again, I will say how important the learning of your earlier lessons are in building a good foundation.

From the time you make the approach to that customer, until you are actually standing there, the customer is subconsciously getting a mental impression of you and the kind of person you are. A customer always puts up an invisible wall of resistance to every new sales situation. That is why we mentioned the fact that your clothing should be tailored and your hair style should be classic. Anything disturbing about your appearance when you are new to someone automatically makes that wall of resistance thicker and harder to break through. So, save your creative dressing for social events with your friends. Even though customers are friends, they are professional friends and they judge you on the basis of acceptable professional codes.

As you are approaching your customers, put a sincere smile on your face. Comfortably and confidently walk up to them. At this time, you, the salesperson, can also be making some mental notes as to something about the business you find unique and good. This observation can be used as an opening along with your greeting to the customer. If it is in a store, perhaps the items are displayed well, or the setting itself is pleasant. If you go into someone's office, many times there are pictures or plaques displayed indicating their interest in a certain hobby. This gives you a perfect opener to say, "Hello, Mr. Customer, I see that you are a fisherman, golfer, baseball player…" This is perfect since you can relate for a few minutes on that topic to put both yourself and your customer at ease. This dialogue is the warm-up stage and should not be rushed. It is the time to topple that wall of resistance that the buyer puts in front of the new salesperson—consciously or not.

This opening move of how to most effectively put customers at ease and make them like you enough to go into the sale is most confusing to a new salesperson. Stop and think a moment about the accomplishments of your friends that make you like them.

* First, they make you feel good about yourself because they accept your talents or good points.

* Second, they are genuinely interested in you and what you have to say.

* Third (and most important) they let you talk about something that is interesting to both you and them.

Why not then greet your new buyer in the same manner of acceptance? We all love to talk about ourselves. So find something about your buyers that interest them and let them talk. When the greeting is complete and the amenities are over, sometimes the salespeople find themselves still standing in the hallway, outer office, or at the center of the store. If this is the case, then ask, yes, ask, the buyer to take you somewhere you would both be most comfortable for a few moments to talk.

When they gesture and at the same time ask you whom you are here to represent and what you want, then start to walk in the direction of that inner office, or even counter space, where you know that buyer is comfortable enough to sit and listen to you for a few minutes. If you are walking toward the order-writing space, you are assuming that the buyer wants to talk to you and he or she does not have to make the choice. You made that choice by going to the order-writing station of the business establishment.

A very important point in making the sale is to remember that sales are not made in the center of the store, where there are a million distractions, or even in the foyers of offices. Try to always go to a space where that buyer is used to doing business. We have discussed the importance of space in another part of this book. People are victims of habit and space used for the specific purpose of order-writing is made habitual by every buyer.

When you have reached the space set aside for the purpose of writing orders, stand and put your briefcase or sample case on the floor while the buyer is being seated. Sit down and prepare to build the second block into the construction of the sale.

As you are preparing to go into the second part of your sale, which is to find the wants and needs of the customer, do not let yourself get involved in the pitfall most inexperienced salespeople fall into. What could that be? You've seen it done in movies. Sometime you see it in training manuals... It is the salesperson handing the customer his or her business card as the approach is made. I say this is wrong for the following reasons. The card is an obstacle at this point; it is not an aid. It is something between the salesperson and the buyer. The card gives the buyer something to focus his or her attention on, just at the critical time when you are trying to capture and keep that buyer's full attention.

Think for a moment about talking to a pipe smoker. That pipe serves a polite way for that person to take his attention away from his visitor and fiddle with his pipe. Your buyer will do the same thing with your card or selling materials. He or she will handle them, read them, put them down, pick them up, and go through all sorts of motions that are distracting to both of you. These motions can break the flow of the sale, especially if you are new to the job. So don't volunteer that card unless it is requested or until your sale is complete. Of course, if you are asked for your card, then you may take it out, but try to hold on to it yourself for a few minutes, until you have finished making an important statement in your greeting and approach. If you have been successful in the approach and greeting, then you will now begin to place the second block of your foundation toward the attainment of your sale.

1. People automatically put up a wall of resistance to a new situation.

2. Visually and verbally try to seem as familiar to the market of people that you are serving as you can.

3. Be sure that the selling process is going on in the space where orders are written.

4. Keep distractions to a minimum during the sales process.

The Best Conversationalists Listen

CHAPTER XI

Learning the Wants and Needs of the Customer

Wants and needs are the first two building blocks most crucial in any sale. If you did your work well in the first part of the sale, the customer now feels more comfortable with you, a new salesperson, and is more willing to be open with you about his or her business. This is the beginning of the transition into the real selling effort. Conversation at this level must be kept on a lively and optimistic note, for it is the interrelating of your selling efforts with the wants and needs of that particular business. At this time you introduce the reason you are there with something factual, yet make it something of interest to that particular buyer about your company. This is when you need to get the buyer's interest stimulated. You want to relate the fact to the buyer that your company, XYZ Corporation, has been manufacturing those things the buyer uses for years and has solved some of the problems associated with the buyer's particular type of business. You can also direct the buyer's attention to your catalogue and you can point out some of the items that you know are generally of interest to people in that type of business.

At this point your statements are generalizations, but they are effective in that you will get feedback from your efforts. This is the time you will hit upon a line of interest from the buyer that you can follow to effectively build your sale. It is at this point that you begin to ask questions and get the customer involved with your products and your company. Keep your conversation enthusiastic about the company and the products and use key phrases such as, "Mr. Customer, what do you think about such and such an idea?" Another is, "That product serves to enhance your business in a particular way. Don't you think so, Mr. Customer?" It is amazing what you will learn when you get that customer to talk.

The next very important thing for you to do at this time is to listen, listen, listen. Remember, you are controlling your sale and the direction in which your sale is going: Whether it goes on that order form, or straight out the window is up to you and the use of your selling technique. If you have gotten the customer to open up to you and tell you some of his or her opinions and problems, then the third building block is practically a cinch. I say practically a cinch for it is only if you have listened and noted in your mind what was important to the buyer that you will be able to locate and present the ideas to fulfill the buyer's needs. Selling is nothing more than feeding back to buyers the solution to the problem they told you they wanted to solve. So we see how one block fits right into the other and builds upon it. Step number three comes just as easily as the first two if you have studied and done your job well.

1. After the introductions and the first exchange between salesperson and buyer, enthusiasm is extremely important in the transference of the selling process.

2. Along with enthusiasm, keeping your buyer's interest is the key to the beginning of a successful outcome of the sale.

3. Ask questions of the buyer. This provides feedback and keeps attention.

4. Control the sale.

Simple Solutions
Achieve The Most

CHAPTER XII

Locating the Tools and Presenting the Sale

Just as easily as every other step has gone right into the next one, so it is with the presentation. It is your job to keep your selling tools so well-organized that it is simple to bring your products to the buyer's attention, at a moment's notice, especially those items that you know will hold the buyer's interest. This is also the time when a little creativity comes onto the scene. The more you know about what your product can do, and the policies of your company, the more creatively you can solve a problem and present an idea. Again, this means that you have had to get a good foundation.

The process of presentation in a creative manner interfaces somewhat like the workings of a computer. You have certain information stored in your mind, such as all you can know about your products and the ideas used successfully before. Then someone (this new buyer) feeds you new information. If you are working your mind in the right way, you will come up with an answer based upon the combination of knowledge offered and stored in your mind. Nine times out of ten, when you use this method, your solutions are tailor-made for that

particular situation and can almost guarantee your
acceptance. That makes your next step 100% easier. Do
your best to stay attentive to the customer through every
part of your sale, so that you will be able to present that
idea or item at the right time. This action brings you
closer to the conclusion of the sale and the signing of
the order.

Always remember when you are presenting your product
line to other people that they will not take the time to search
for what they are looking for. Therefore, you want to have
your materials and selling aids available and organized at all
times. Such forethought enables you to bring these items to
the attention of a busy buyer with a minimum of movement
and effort. This is important as the buyer's attention can
easily be lost at this point if you are fumbling in your
briefcase, looking for the sample, price, or brochure that you
knew was there last month. Be ready, be organized, and go
over your materials each night when you go home, to be
sure that everything is in its proper place and that you have
all of the materials you need for the following day.

To summarize, the keys to properly locating and
presenting the line are knowledge, creativity, organization
and attention. If you use those four traits when you are
out there, presenting your product or your ideas, then they
will be truly unique and generally acceptable. Remember,
going back to our lessons on the foundation of the sale,

the buyer will give the order to the sales rep, who quickly and efficiently presents the idea or item that makes the purchaser want to buy. You will learn what everyone looks for in buying anything in the next chapter. If the presentation is successful, your sale is practically guaranteed and will come easily if you have studied and done your job well.

1. Offer solutions to the customer's dilemmas with your product and/or service.

2. Creativity in problem solving will help one salesperson make a sale that another could not complete.

3. Be organized so that you can stay attentive to your customer.

People don't commit to anything

unless they invest... time... money!

CHAPTER XIII

Put Sizzle into Your Sale

Now that you have gotten this far, the customer is interested and has given you hints as to what he or she needs and will buy. You can now present what you have to fulfill the need that was created or the solution to the problem that was stated by the buyer. I am going to repeat the phrase—the need that was created—when you learned the wants and needs of your customer. This is very important to know, for most of the time a good salesperson creates the need for the service or product by using word pictures to create the dream. The sizzle is the picture of the fulfillment of that dream.

Children are best at selling the "sizzle" to their parents or teachers. The pink dress with the sparkly, shiny, gold trim and the shiny, black shoes your daughter wants you to buy for her are not just a dress and shoes. It is an outfit that will transform her into a princess. It is the princess part that she will sell to you. What about the new baseball glove your son wants? It is not just a baseball glove; it is the thing that will transform him into a champion on the playing field.

Today when so many messages are thrown at us from so many different directions, customers will not seek out your product or service without you showing how it would benefit them. Build the dream with the perfect product or service to fulfill the need. After the dream is built, it is your job to show the customer how to buy the service or product from you. If the desire to buy was stimulated effectively enough, then the customer will make the conviction to exchange dollars for your product or service.

To stimulate the desire to exchange dollars to buy from you, the salesperson, you must know your product line or service benefits so well that you use the benefits at the right moment. Sometimes it takes more than one try to close the customer. On average a person needs to be asked five times to complete a transaction. You can use different closes each time. You then must show the customer how the product or service will help them achieve any of the things people generally want when they purchase anything. When this is done effectively, the sale is almost a guarantee.

Certainly there are general reasons why people buy anything. Those things that people wish to achieve when they buy anything are as follows:

1. To Gain... They may want love, respect, prestige, health, or even a better way of life for themselves.

2. To Be Recognized... as a good fellow, important person, or even a good parent. Can your product or service help them to do that? Perhaps it can make them feel more important because it can make them more successful.

3. To Express Themselves and Be Like People Who Are Successful ... Who in that person's business would this buyer like to imitate? Has that person used the idea or item that you are selling to this new account? If so, mention that for it almost always makes a sale, but do be honest, or you will never sell that customer anything again. If you lie at this point, when you are new to a market, then your job will be made twice as hard for you.

4. To Save ... Can your product or service save time, money, work, or convenience for that buyer or that company? If so, say how specifically and in detail. Maybe someone else in their field is using this method to do the same thing and is saving time by doing so. Be sure to talk about this.

It sounds easy huh? It is only easy if you memorize and use one or more of the above criteria in each and every sale you make. There is a formula for success in anything. The formula that applies here is as follows: Where the lines of knowledge and timing meet =

SUCCESS. You have to be ready when this interfacing does occur, for if you don't know when this happens, then you would have to be very lucky to achieve anything. Study and work hard, pay attention to your job, and bring the opportunity for success.

To summarize, I want you to keep in mind the same word that is used over and over in this book. That is to SERVE ... You are out there in sales to serve the needs and desires of your customers. I have just given you four of the greatest secrets to know in sales. If you know why people buy generally and you use your selling skills well, then you can achieve twice as much and accumulate a fortune.

1. Learn why anyone buys anything.

2. Listen and learn why the particular person you are selling to will buy.

3. The good salesperson makes the sale happen.

Timing...

The moment gone
is never recaptured...

Only prefabricated!

CHAPTER XIV

Close the Sale

This is another critical and extremely important part of successful salesmanship. Do you want to know another secret? There are a lot of very rich and successful salespeople in the world, who may not be strong in any other part of the sale other than the close. The reason for their success is that there are many times in the sequence of a sale that the closing signals are given for a salesperson to recognize.

A good closer knows just what each and every one of those signals are and closes immediately each time the buying signal is given to him or her. The closing is an integral part of the entire selling process and there are many verbal and nonverbal buying signals. The most obvious signal of a close is when a customer further questions and dwells on an item or an idea. At this time the buyers may ask about costs, delivery times, or availability. When this occurs do your best to write on your order form what the buyer is asking you about. At this point when you want a commitment, give a customer a choice between two ideas, two items, or two delivery times. This is a psychological and very subtle way of asking the customer for a commitment to buy. Almost every time the customers will make the choice knowing full well that they have made the commitment to buy, without anyone ever having to make the decision.

Remember, in selling the question is not of buying, but when to deliver the product and how much. Also, keep in mind that a good salesperson controls the sale. When you give choices, make sure that either choice the buyer makes is to the advantage of the sale. Sometimes the buyer gives a verbal buying signal by asking the questions that you learned in the previous part of these lessons. The question may be a direct reference to the general motivation that makes people buy anything.

The customer may just come right out and ask you who else in the industry uses the products you are selling or they may ask in another way how they can gain from using your idea or product. These questions are put to the salesperson in a subtle manner, such as, "Do you advertise your product?" Another question in direct motivational selling could be, "If the cost of your service or product is higher initially, are there longterm benefits to be derived from using this product or service?" These are just two examples of the many verbal buying signals that are not overtly stated, but they are leading questions showing the customer's interest in buying from the salesperson. When they occur they should be followed up quickly by a close from the salesperson.

Your job in sales is to sell your product or service as quickly and efficiently as possible. The best way to do this is to recognize and seize opportunity quickly and to act upon it. Another key phrase for all salespeople to remember is to get the job done. "DO IT NOW!" This is especially appropriate in the closing of a sale. The key to successful closing in any sale is not to wait for the next phase of questioning, or the next presentation, but to close the sale immediately after receiving the buying signal.

How important were those techniques that you learned early in regard to etiquette and the simple rules of interacting with people? Very. Use them right now when you are in the middle of making your sale and are out in the middle of the sea, so to speak; when you are all alone. The idea of being attentive and polite is admirable. Staying attentive during the entire sale (and that means during every sequence of the sale), is brought home to you right now. There are many nonverbal buying signals to denote that it is time to close the sale. In order to close sales successfully, you must be aware of changes in a buyer's facial expressions, such as a smile, or a look of interest at a particular item. Perhaps their hands linger on a certain phrase or item in a catalogue or their glance may be held for a length of time that appears uncommon. These are very definite buying

signals. The inexperienced salesperson finds these
changes at times too subtle to detect.

Unless, and I repeat, unless, he or she is paying close
attention all through the sale, the salesperson may just let
these subtle buying signals pass and lose the sale. More
often than you might think, at the same time you get the
buying signal, which you recognize as an opportunity to
close, you will also get feedback from the customer
asking for more time. The customer may verbally ask
you to wait, or use a nonverbal ploy, such as walking
away from the order-writing space to another part of the
room. This movement means that the customer wants a
few minutes to reinforce his or her own conviction to
buy.

By all means, let the customer have this time. However,
this is not the time for you, the salesperson, to stand
there looking bored and disinterested. What you should
be doing at this time is helping your customer make the
decision by going over the points of the product or the
idea that appealed to that buyer in the first place. Now
you are narrowing the selections and options to a
minimum, but are enthusiastically keeping the major
selling points in the customer's mind. Usually this works
like magic. However, there are times when the buyer
wants more conviction. If you were smart, you thought
of some more selling points or are rephrasing those

major selling points you used in the first place. Always try to keep something in mind that you can use should you get into a bind when you are so close to making the sale.

Earlier we stated that a good salesperson never rushes a buyer, yet can always leave with a signed order and a buyer happy with his or her purchase. When you know how to do these things, then you are, beyond any doubt, on your way to being the most successful salesperson in your organization. Again, the two most important things in closing a sale is not "If" your customer wants to buy, but "When to deliver" and "How much".

To summarize: A smooth closing demonstrates that the salesperson did not rush the buyer, but instead, kept using strong selling points until the buyer made a happy decision to buy that particular product or service. Why must customers always be happy that they bought from a particular salesperson? It's simple; you've heard it a thousand times: Happy customers always return and they tell other people about you and your product or service. Repeat business is the way successful salespeople earn top dollars.

The qualities of character, such as honesty, integrity, and hard work, coupled with developed skills in salesmanship, cannot help but lead you to success. Those days of the peddler pulling a fast one on the customer are gone. Buyers and business people are too sophisticated and too busy today to put up with false showmanship. High quality, developed skills and excellent products cause salespeople to stay successful in this decade and in those decades that will follow.

We have discussed how to close a sale. However, sometimes a salesperson has spent his or her time and gas dollars to see an account and the account refuses to let the sale go beyond the creating the need part of the sale. What do you, the new salesperson, or any salesperson, do in a situation such as this? This is a crucial point in the sequence of the sale and something that happens even to the best of salespeople. You have taken the time to build four blocks of the sale and have done this painstakingly by using your ideas and tailoring a program just for that particular account.

An old joke between salespeople was to find the competitor's new salespeople and follow them around. Why would you want to do that, do you think? The inexperienced sales rep plays right into the traps set by the customer. Just at the time when you, as a salesperson, are feeling so sure of your ability to secure the order, the customer may throw a devastating pitfall into your path. This happens to all of us, not just the inexperienced salesperson. Do you want to know what that pitfall is and what to do about it? There are at least six times a day, every day, when a salesperson will spend time with an account and the buyer just doesn't want to make a decision, so the buyer asks a question: The one make-or-break sales question. That question is, "When will you [the salesperson] be back that way again?"

This is an obvious attempt to put off making the decision, or altering the conviction to exchange dollars for product. Again, the difference between the successful professional and the inexperienced salesperson resides in the way problems are handled when they arise. The inexperienced salesperson falls right into the trap by answering the question just as the buyer expects. That is, the salesperson will say, "I'll be back in two weeks, or two months, etc."

The obvious reply by the customer is, "Good, I'll definitely buy from you the next time you come in to see me." If the industry is a competitive one (and what industry isn't today), then that particular salesperson will leave before the sale is closed and a sharp competitor will walk in to see the account two hours or two days later and close an easy sale. Why? Because the idea of using that particular product was stored subconsciously in the customer's mind. When the idea is presented to the customer again by a competitor, the desire to buy had already been created previously, but the sale was not completed or in sales language, "closed." All that the new salesperson has to do at this point is to recognize the interest of the buyer and close the sale.

After using all that time and energy building your sale, do not leave the account without making a sale of some kind, even if it has to be a small one. A very important point in the game of selling is whether you think you have won the sale or not. Do not leave until the goal of writing some type of order is achieved. Often times, when new salespeople leave an account without securing an order the first couple of times, they will never sell that account anything in the future either.

Many responses in situations are habits. If a salesperson can make it a habit that when he or she walks into a business or a shop to sell something that he or she walks out with an order, then as long as that sales rep calls on that particular buyer, the same positive result will occur. Conversely, if the sales rep leaves the buyer more than once without writing an order, then nine times out of ten, this same negative result will keep recurring. That buyer will never purchase anything from that particular salesperson. In order to circumvent the problem of the delayed sale, the following responses work:

1.   "Mr. Customer, my territory is very large, and it is important for me to reach as many people as I can in a

day in order to sell these fine products. If you buy today, Mr. Customer, you will have what you need, just at the time when you need to have it." (You are reminding him or her to do it NOW.)

2. "Mr. Customer, I know how busy you are. That's why I would like for you to try my product NOW, so you will be able to see how much it can do for your business."

3. "Mr. Customer, with gas prices the way they are today, if I came back to every one of my customers, I would be out of business before the week was out." (Laugh at this point; make it a joke.) "Let's try the product NOW, to save the expense of my coming back and my taking up any more of your valuable time."

The above are only a few examples; you may think of a few that suit your own style better. The main point to remember here is not to be put off if you can possibly help it.

Close your sale at the earliest possible time. If there is some reason that you simply cannot close the sale (perhaps the customer has an appointment and is in a rush), then it is your responsibility still to remain courteous and pleasant. If the reason is that the customer has an appointment, then make plans with that customer for you to come back later that day or that week. If it is another reason, then leave your card, and leave an idea in the mind of your customer by going over strong selling points, which are unique only to your company. Often a buyer is fair enough to return a call to a courteous and attentive sales rep, having remembered the particular product. Even better, you, the salesperson, could follow up and get an order written for a later delivery.

To summarize, the close is an integral part of the entire selling process. The close should be acted upon and completed when the buyer gives either verbal or non-verbal buying signals. Study this material on the close of the sale until you have memorized it: Knowing when to close, and DOING IT NOW, adds up to lots of dollars in the salesperson's pocket. So, stay alert and close the sale quickly.

1. Good salespeople always try to close a sale as quickly as possible.

2. There are many ways to ask for a completion to the sale and the good salesperson uses many different and effective closing phrases.

3. If the response to the attempts to close are not what you, the salesperson, want, then go over the good points of the sale as many times as it takes to get an affirmative response to the sale.

4. Don't force the sale prematurely, but do press for the close.

5. Don't leave a promising sales situation unless you absolutely have to.

**Brevity
is the
essence
of
interest.**

CHAPTER XV

Add on to the Sale

Many times a phrase is continuously repeated in this series of lessons. The idea that selling is a continuous process that does not end when the order is signed is no exception. If you can think of something that you know the customer was interested in and didn't buy while you were writing the order, then mention it. The worst thing that can happen is that the customer will want to buy it when you return and the best that can happen is that it will be added on to the order you have already written. If you, as a salesperson, have done your job successfully and well and your customer is happy at having been smart enough to buy from you, the successful salesperson, then the customer will not object to having his or her interest piqued further by an exceptional idea or product.

It is simple to add on to the sale you have just completed while you are still there. Discuss new ideas, new ways to use other products in your line. Of course, this is after you have that customer's signature on the order you have just written. Then if the customer seems interested, take out another order form (not the one just signed) and add on to what you have already sold. I've seen salespeople do this with each and every order written and earn themselves an extra five or six hundred dollars just in add-on business. The customer is most vulnerable when his or her defensiveness is gone and that is just after a sale is successfully completed.

You must also use your head in making the decision as to whether or not you can successfully add to your sale. Sometimes the sale has been an exceptionally long and tedious one and the customer has been pushed to the limits of his or her attention span. In that case simply give hints and ideas about what can be ordered next time. Then give your sincere thanks for this order and leave.

You will be surprised when you return to that account and the customer recalls some of the things that you mentioned previously. Try to add on to the sale and try to hold the interest of the customer, but be perceptive enough to know when you have used up his or her attention span. If this has happened, then say, "Thank You" and exit. Even if you did not get to add to the sale, you were able to do a little advertising. Remember, good advertising works on a subconscious as well as a conscious level. Each and every time that you give a thought or an idea to be considered over a period of time, you are doing a little subconscious advertising. Always leave a hint about when you will return. This sticks in the customer's mind and after you have been selling to that account for a while, you will be surprised to learn that any deviation in your schedule is noticed and commented on by the account.

Especially if you are new to your sales job, be reliable. As I stated before, good salesmanship is akin to the constant courteous qualities of character an individual has. So, be reliable and be honest. These two traits of character may make up for a lot of errors you may make in your first few sales.

1. Add on to the sale that you have just made. It is far easier to work with a situation that you know than to try to open up an entirely new one.

2. If you cannot add on to the sale you just made, then advertise the next one that you will make to that buyer.

3. Do what you said you would do.

Walk that extra mile.

Know what few know,

and

go where few go!

CHAPTER XVI

The Follow-Up to the Sale

Selling is visible, verbal, and tangible just as much as it is impressionistic and non-verbal. If more people knew that retentive memory of the buyer greatly attributed to the success or failure of many salespeople, then the salesperson would have an insight that would streamline the job even further. When you, the salesperson, have left that buyer's premises, you have left him or her with a picture of you, your presentation, and your — it was courteous and honest, or disinterested and vague. Not only is that impression that you made etched in the mind of the buyer, but also that sale that you made is there also. Were you willing to let buyers be completely convinced how smart they were in purchasing from you? Were you willing to go over each and every good point that came out in the selling process to help these buyers establish their conviction to buy? If you have done the aforementioned, then your follow-up will absolutely guarantee you a second sale. Sometimes this is immediately after the account receives the first order. That extra little minute that a salesperson takes to phone a new account, knowing full well that delivery has been made on the order, to ask if the customer has any questions or concerns, can be the making of either a fast reorder, or a larger reorder the second time you see the customer.

If you don't want to phone, print on a postal card a few words about when you will return to see the account, as well as your hopes that they are pleased with the product that you have sold him or her. Your rating will go up 100% with this account when you show that extra little effort. In addition, your finances will soar. The reason for this escalation can be summed up in one little word: CARE. You have shown that you care about your job, your selling efforts, and your customer.

This showing that your job is important to you instills confidence in you from other people. That is what you were striving for in every block you built toward a successful sale. You were building confidence that you, as a salesperson, would be able to serve their needs, as well as anyone who had sold to them before. When you give your time, your effort, and your skill in doing your job freely and happily, then people return that effort to you tenfold. You inspire the same feelings in others that you wish to give.

1. Always keep in touch with your customers.

2. Reinforce the conviction that the customer made the right choice in buying from you by showing courtesy and care.

3. Be attentive and honest with your customers.

SUMMARY

The above seven building blocks are not comprised of anything that we have not heard before. They are really showing that courtesy and integrity can help you in anything you do in life. These good qualities of character must be part of every salesperson. Anything that an individual is a part of—be it family, community, or organization—that individual's willingness to serve and care determines the success and growth for the entire group. Even if you read and study these lessons and never go out to sell, it makes good sense to have an awareness of what determines the success or failure in interactions between human beings. That, after all, is what living in our world today is all about.

PART III: Exercises and Conclusion

As technology advances,
man must gain more mastery
over himself!

...he called upon his brain to
see who would answer.

CHAPTER XVII

How to use the Telephone

Okay, I know what you are thinking. Now I have completely used up your patience and I am beginning to insult you as well! Of course, you know how to use the telephone—we all learned that when we were just toddlers exploring our world. However, remember back a few chapters, when we began to realize that we do everything we do out of habit? Most of the time when we answer a telephone, our mind is still on what we were doing before we answered the call. We are more into ourselves when we talk on a telephone than at any other time in our relating to other people. Part of the reason for this is the artificial barrier that most of us feel the telephone provides. In another part of this book, we touched upon the idea that we, as humans, hold claim to certain space. A telephone can be an artificial barrier, as it is an object between two individuals holding a conversation. When we have barriers around us, then we feel very powerful. Sometimes people can get carried away on the telephone and make some irresponsible statements. Some things can be agreed to on the telephone that individuals never intended to honor with any action. Individuals think they are not in the real world because no one is visibly near. The person feels protected by a false zone of privacy and is a little less true in what he or she says.

Therefore, an experienced salesperson will quickly make an appointment time to follow up a sales conversation as soon as possible so he or she may be able to get his or her signed order or contract right away. Understanding and making note of this information lets us go on the premise that Alexander Graham Bell did a wonderful thing for salespeople by providing them with a device that lets them canvas a territory for prospective buyers easily and quickly. The other parts of this book have covered all areas of visual selling by checking grooming, approach, presentation, and so forth. Now it is time to project verbally as well.

Since we realize that we do almost everything out of habit, then before we can go on with this section of the book, we must indulge ourselves by participating in an important exercise. You will be surprised at some of the things you do when you either talk on or answer a telephone. For the next 24 hours, really watch how you answer the telephone and how you relate to other people when you are talking on the telephone. It is most important at this time to really listen. Listen to the voice inflections: The tone lets you know a lot about the mood and interest you are getting on the other end of that line.

If you have never done an exercise such as this one, then you will first be amazed about yourself and how well you project on the telephone, but most importantly, what you can sensorily pick up from the other party on that line. This exercise would be much like selling to someone in person if you could not see them, for you would have an awareness of someone being in front of you, but feeling that awareness and not seeing anyone. In order to effectively communicate, you would have to completely get out of yourself and free your mind of any predetermined thoughts or phrases. At this time you must really concentrate so that you can gear your responses to the mood, tone, and concepts of the other person. Failure to do so is the main reason why most of us are not as effective in a telephone sales situation as we should be. We all try to outguess a situation and are not aware of the other person's needs and desires.

I have seen grown men try to train themselves to use the telephone to sell, who end up getting so frustrated that they pretty nearly yank the telephone from the wall. Remember when we talked about how you create an image with your manner and appearance? Then we showed how the person you wanted to sell something to had mentally decided whether or not to give you his or her time and attention, even before you ever said anything? Well, via telephone, you have exactly seven, yes, seven seconds to get your party's attention. It is well to remember in this seven second interval to be direct, informative and clear about what you want. Most salespeople will hedge and say cutesy things thinking this will mellow the person at the other end of that telephone line. Actually, the reverse happens. The person at the other end of the line becomes impatient and a little annoyed. The caller is then at a disadvantage: If that caller states the reason for calling right away, then the chances are much better that the buyer's attention will be attracted and the caller will stay in control.

In that seven second interval, you, the seller, must identify yourself, get a response from the party you are calling and give out a catchy phrase that is so inviting the prospective buyer cannot help but be hanging onto the line impatiently awaiting further word from you. That is quite a chore today when we are overloaded with so much information from so many different sources. Remember, we are practicing, and you are allowing a 24 hour period for this exercise so that you can effectively observe everything you do when you answer or make a telephone call.

How quickly can your mind become attuned to the caller when you answer the telephone? How well do you listen to the other person? While the other party is talking, does your mind wander to a thousand other things that need to be done? Or, are you thinking of what you want to say next, without listening effectively to the other person? Really make yourself listen during this time. Listen to the tone of the other person's voice. Is it bored, interested, enthusiastic, or someplace else? Try to change any disinterest that your ear picks up to enthusiasm by using your tone of voice or a thought suggestion that would bring the person on the other end of the line to think of what you want them to consider.

Remember, moods, deeds, pictures, and even accomplishments, are thoughts first. Whether we use words or gestures, deeds or pictures to start these thought processes depends upon our situation. In the instance of selling on the telephone the use of words to make thought pictures and to set a mood is most important. An example of setting a mood via words would be how you go about introducing yourself. In your opening you could say something like, "Mr. Jones, isn't it a wonderful rainy day? We've needed these showers for a long time."

The wrong way to do this would be saying in your introduction, "How are you, Mr. Jones? Yes, I know that it's raining again." The second phrase automatically sets up a gloomy mood. So, especially on the phone, it is most important that you keep your voice and your thoughts centered on a high level of optimism. The tones of peoples' voices are a sure giveaway as to whether they are successful and optimistic, or anxious and gloomy. In the area of telephone sales, using pictures painted by words is the only way to effectively set a mood and get an idea across.

Remember, we are doing an exercise, where you will watch yourself and your telephone manners for a 24 hour period. No one else needs to know what you are doing. Practice this well, for if you can effectively master yourself first, then you are well on your way to increasing your sales production by at least an extra 50%. This does not even take into account the amount of money that can be saved on gas or in time. So, during this 24 hour period do not try to judge yourself: Just spend the time watching as you would watch another caller. Only you know what you do right 90% of the time. The only way that we can be completely honest with ourselves is to realize that we have a goal to achieve by changing ineffective, bad, perhaps even rude, verbal habits into productive and pleasant, as well as courteous and hopeful, ways of communicating.

Now you have an idea of what you do when you either answer a telephone or make a call. What about how you communicate and sound to another when you use the telephone? Why not try calling a trusted friend, mother, brother, or husband and use your best telephone personality to sell them your product, idea, or concept?

Take another 24 hour period to just practice this. You saw how effective the previous 24 hour practice was for you. Now you can spend 24 more hours in self-evaluation and self-improvement. If you can be your own best friend, so to speak, and can talk into a recording machine at first, then do so until you come up with a sales style that you think is convincing enough. Now you can try this on someone else. Talking to a friend or family member is sometimes a lot harder than talking to a total stranger. So do be easier on yourself by practicing the first five or six sales pitches on the recording machine. Then try the perfected sales technique on a member of your family or a friend. They will like you better for it, too.

In the previous 24 hour period, you should have gotten an idea of how you communicate and where you need to practice. At first, just concentrate on making your voice effective by being enthusiastic and try speaking clearly. Remember immediately to identify yourself. You then want to get the other person into a situation where they have to respond to a question. When you have done this, then go into a phrase that would be termed an attention getter. An example of this would be, "Mr. Jones, this new process gives you a prestigious and popular product at a very economical price." The attention getter makes the listener pause and focus his or her mind on what you are saying long enough for you to go into the explanation of yourself and your product. It eventually lets you set up an appointment time to see the prospective buyer. If you are using friends or family members at this time, then let them critique your attention grabber line, and see if it can be better. Also, let them tell you if your tone of voice was pleasant and enthusiastic.

You may want to go back to the recording machine and practice again. The reason that the recording machine is good is that you will be more creative and freer in your approach than you would be if you knew someone was either going to criticize you or laugh if you make some mistakes. Also, this little machine lets you listen to your own tone of voice so you know what the person on the other end of the telephone is hearing.

If the quality and tone of your voice are not up to par, then you should take the time to practice on the recording machine until you think your own voice is pleasant to hear. Why not? People in the theatre or on the radio do it as their voice is their livelihood. Isn't yours the same thing in telephone sales? A good, strong resonance, coupled with a happy, enthusiastic air, and good, clear concise enunciation is what you should be aiming for. Remember, you are going to do this for at least another 24 hour period.

After you have done this, then it is time to call that prospective customer or client. See how effective you are in setting the mood of the conversation, getting the customer's interest, and closing with an appointment or order? It is at this time that you will get an idea of the barriers that will be placed in front of you as objections to closing either the sale or the appointment time. This is the time you really have to let the other person talk. You must really listen, not only to words, but to tone and mood.

Now is the time to learn one of the most effective communication styles that has proven to bring results. It is a very simple thing, yet most people never use this simple maneuver: This is the pause. ... Most people are nervous when they use the telephone simply because they never had to learn to be effectively aware of the person on the other end of the line. You have probably noticed in those little exercises that you completed that pcoplc, cvcn important, impressive people, talk too loudly and too fast on the telephone.

The pause will slow you down and make your speaking more emphatic. Pausing is especially good when you are trying to make a statement of fact that provides impact. This little pause after an important statement causes the person on the other end of the line to let down some of those artificial barriers and to open some type of communication with you. In other words, you can possibly get some feedback at this point by using the pause. That is a very important thing, for it provides the basis on which to proceed with your line of thought and the selling trend you were following. If you didn't have a selling lead-in before, then at this time you can get a clue as to where to put the most emphasis. Remember, when making a lead into your selling phase, make your statement of fact with the greatest amount of impact and use the pause. Do not he afraid of it. The pause lets you gather your thoughts and go into your sale with more feedback from your customer.

Now that your introduction and approach have been made, it is time to go into the sale itself. Talk slowly, confidently, and concisely when you are explaining and selling. Make as many major statements of fact as you possibly can and emphasize these with effective pauses. If you need feedback at certain intervals, then pause and ask your customer what he or she thinks. Remember, be clear and direct and use as few unimportant words as possible.

For example, let's say you are selling real estate and you have just found the property that your client is looking for. In your most enthusiastic and clear voice discuss the major features of the property. Explain how it is a good financial investment and why. At this point, pause. Then tell of the location features and the future growth potential of this area, then pause again. Perhaps, at the second pause, you will ask for feedback from the person on the other end of the line. To do this you might say something like, "Mr. Jones, isn't it grand that we have located the property in the very location and at the very price that you were looking for?" Now the pause, then get that response from your client. Keep the client engaged on the major selling points. In doing this some people will sell themselves on an idea. If that happens, then it is time for the salesperson to hear the buy signal and close the sale.

The attention span of a buyer, or a potential buyer, is much shorter on the telephone than it is in person. Be sure that you are able to include all of your major phrases of fact and impact in a sales pitch that takes no longer than three . . . that's right .. . three minutes. That is the right amount of time for your customer to absorb what you have to say and it gives enough time to let them mentally absorb your idea concept. After your three minute sales pitch, give the customer a question time. If they do not question you, then you question them.

For example, let's say you have just told your potential customer of a new concept in wall decor and have described the size, materials, and installation technique.

This is the time for the customer to ask you about price, different motifs of design, etc. If the customer, at this point, is still not convinced, then go back over three major phrases of impact. An example of this might be, "Mr. Jones, by purchasing this particular concept, you will save time and money because of the ease of choice and delivery." Then deliberately pause, and check the tone and modulation of your voice. You can begin to talk more slowly at this point to really emphasize your selling points. Also, be sure that your voice shows a good amount of confidence. If you don't sound fully convinced that your product is the best there is, then you certainly won't convince someone else that it is.

Use as many adjectives as you can to form pictures in the mind of the other person. For example, you can say, "Mr. Jones, this particular technique gives a three-dimensional feel to the wall-hanging, and the colors create a vibrant mood because of their vivid hues." Practice thinking in terms of word pictures and make notes of as many as you can think of. Practice this as often as possible. Remember, the rewards are great when you master this.

I know you are thinking that it is going to be almost impossible to master a great sales pitch, keep the customer's attention, and check on your own voice to be sure that it shows friendliness and confidence. All of these coordinating effects are going to feel mighty awkward at first. However, if you really want to be good at telephone sales, the rewards are great, but only if you practice every day. Before the training week is over, you will begin to see the first smooth sales talk begin to happen to you.

If you have ever tried to master a sport where you had to act and think of your every move at the same time, the telephone exercise is the same thing. If the sport you were trying to master was tennis, for instance, you would probably keep misplacing the return ball just so you could concentrate on hitting it. Eventually, you would be able to place the ball where you wanted it to go, once you learned how to coordinate your strokes.

A great part of success is the visualization in your own mind of your achieving the training goal that you set for yourself. While you are training yourself for selling on the telephone, picture in your mind all of your customers saying, "Yes, that is a wonderful idea, I want to buy that from you." See yourself giving a smooth, friendly and effective sales talk. Then see the signed order or contract. What a difference this will make in your productivity because your mental attitude will be so super charged!

Mental attitude is the real secret to being a successful anything. Being hopeful, cheerful, and expecting success will help you accomplish any goal you wish for yourself. Keep those two words in your mind through anything you wish to achieve. They can be the most powerful tools that we have. Remember to EXPECT SUCCESS.

You have come so far already in mastering not only the telephone, but yourself as well. Eventually, this telephone, which was such an alien instrument before, will be like a child's toy for you. It will become an effective tool that you have mastered and it will work for you to gain you riches and success. It is important that we all learn to use the best technology in communicating no matter what our vocation, for we will be forced to communicate through some type of media.

If you have absorbed, practiced, and learned the facts set down in the pages of this book, then you are well on your way to achieving riches and success, while being as independent as you can make yourself. This is what surviving in the times to come will necessitate.

1. Listen, really listen, to the call to get the feedback that comes from the other end of the telephone line.

2. The caller has seven seconds to catch the interest of the person on the other end of the telephone.

3. Be direct to show strength of conviction on the telephone. Hedging shows lack of conviction and weakness.

4. Instead of visually watching for signs of interest, you must truly listen for them.

5. Moods are brought out in voice, tone and inflection much more on the telephone than in person.

6. Pause during telephone conversations to give impact and conviction to your sale.

7. Ask questions that require more than just "yes" and "no" answers on the telephone.

8. Use word pictures for telephone selling.

CHAPTER XVIII

The Assignment and the Assessment

After all, selling is goal setting. In order to be successful in the game of sales one must set daily, monthly, and yearly goals. Visualize yourself reaching one goal a week. Perform an exercise of visualization each morning before going about your selling career. For ten minutes each morning concentrate on the following goals and stay with one goal for a week at a time.

Visualize yourself:

Perfectly groomed and dressed like the most successful salesperson in your field.

Having each and every person that you go to see waiting for you openly with a smile... genuinely glad to see you!

Servicing each and every account in which a sale was completed by sending a post card or calling to say that you appreciate their business and asking if there is anything you can do for them NOW?

Having the dollar amount you wish to sell on each of your signed orders.

Having each sale you attempt brought to a successful close.

Feeling... HAPPY... CONTENT... SUCCESSFUL!

Being all of the above... starting ... NOW!

CHAPTER XIX

Conclusion

The ideas and actions that have been set to paper on these pages are not just words that have been thought up to make the pages full. Each and every idea and action has been lived and practiced. These formulas have been proven to work, for they have been used over and over again until they are part of the complete psyche of this salesperson. That is what I want each and every one of you to do. Make the words on these pages a living thing. Go out into your own world and build your own success by whatever inspiration you gained from these ideas.

In conclusion, I will quote a poem that was written by Edgar A. Guest. If anything sums up the attitude that brings success in selling and in business, then it would be these words:

GOOD BUSINESS
By Edgar A. Guest

If I possessed a shop or store

I'd drive the grouches off my floor

I'd never let some gloomy guy offend the

Folks who come to buy!

I'd never keep a boy or clerk

With mental toothache at his work

Nor let a man who draws my pay

Drive customers of mine away;

I'd treat the man who takes my time

And spends a nickel or a dime

With a courtesy, and make him feel

That I was pleased to close the deal.

Because, tomorrow, who can tell?

He may want stuff I have to sell

And in that case, then glad he'll be

To spend his dollars all with me...

The reason people pass one door

To patronize another store...

Is not because the busier place

Has better silks or gloves or lace

Or special prices, but it lies

In pleasant words, and smiling eyes;

The only difference, I believe

IS IN THE TREATMENT FOLKS
RECEIVE!

©1981 Prophecy Jewelry Co.

About the Author

Sheryl Green has been an award-winning sales professional for over thirty years. Her experience covers many aspects of sales, including advertising, wholesale, retail, and real estate. Her success in all of these areas has been achieved by applying the principles set forth in this book. Sheryl can be contacted at: sherylgreensells@gmail.com